CC

THOMAS CRANE PUBLIC LIBRARY
QUINCY MASS
CITY APPROPRIATION

MOVIE STAR

LISA REGAN

WINDMILL BOOKS™
New York

Published in 2013 by Windmill Books, An Imprint of Rosen Publishing
29 East 21st Street, New York, NY 10010

Produced for Windmill by Calcium Creative Ltd
Editors for Calcium Creative Ltd: Sarah Eason and Vicky Egan
US Editor: Sara Antill
Designer: Nick Leggett

Cover: Dreamstime: Anpet2000 fg, JStudio 9; Shutterstock: Rafael Ramirez Lee bg. Inside: Istockphoto: Digital Planet Design 27, Lovleah 3, Twin City Chick 5; Shutterstock: AISPIX by Image Source 20, Sam Aronov 7, Aspen Rock 28, Cheryl Casey 23, Creatista 8, 10, 18, 21, Jaimie Duplass 13, Helga Esteb 25, 26, 29, Elena Elisseeva 12, Mandy Godbehear 22, 24, Karamysh 14, Rob Marmion 4, Niderlander 11, OtnaYdur 15, Slavoljub Pantelic 1, Joe Seer 16, 17, SergiyN 19, Jaren Jai Wicklund 6.

Library of Congress Cataloging-in-Publication Data

Regan, Lisa, 1971–
 Movie star / by Lisa Regan.
    p. cm. — (Stage school)
 Includes Index.
 ISBN 978-1-4488-8095-9 (library binding) — ISBN 978-1-4488-8154-3 (pbk.)
 — ISBN 978-1-4488-8160-4 (6-pack)
 1. Motion picture acting—Vocational guidance—Juvenile literature. I. Title.
 PN1995.9.A26R44 2013
 791.4302'8023—dc23
                              2012052810

Manufactured in the United States of America

CPSIA Compliance Information: Batch #B3S12WM: For Further Information contact Windmill Books, New York, New York at 1-866-478-0556

CONTENTS

MAKING MOVIES

Do you look at a movie screen and wish it were you up there? Well, it's time to stop dreaming and start acting!

Making it

To become a movie star you will need to have great acting skills, be willing to take part in lots of **auditions** to get parts, and be determined to succeed. Remember, many successful actors spent years playing small parts in movies before they got their first starring role.

⇦ *Movies are magical. Wouldn't you love to be in one?*

Lucky break

Some young actors do get parts in movies, but don't expect to be a star right away. You are far more likely to start out by getting a bit part in a TV **commercial** or show. If you put in a lot of hard work, with luck you may get a big break into movies!

Radcliffe and Grint

Child actors start out in different ways. Daniel Radcliffe had appeared on TV and in a movie before he got the part of Harry Potter. Rupert Grint had only appeared in his school play before he was cast as Ron Weasley.

⇦ *Lots of stage school students want a piece of the action in movies!*

HOLLYWOOD
PRODUCTION
DIRECTOR
CAMERA
DATE   SCENE   TAKE

GOT WHAT IT TAKES?

Don't kid yourself! Being a movie actor isn't easy. It means early mornings and late nights. Then you'll have to get up the next day and do it all over again! You'll also spend long hours "in makeup" (having your makeup put on), or waiting for your turn in front of the camera.

⇦ *Young stars have to fit in school studies whenever they can.*

Have you got what it takes?

To be an actor, you'll have to learn lots of lines and follow instructions from the director 100 percent of the time.

School days

Filming days can be long. It is still important for child actors to continue their education while they're working, so they have their own teacher, or tutor, on set.

⬆ *Child star Daniel Radcliffe was taught for four hours on set each day during the filming of the Harry Potter movies.*

ACT THE PART

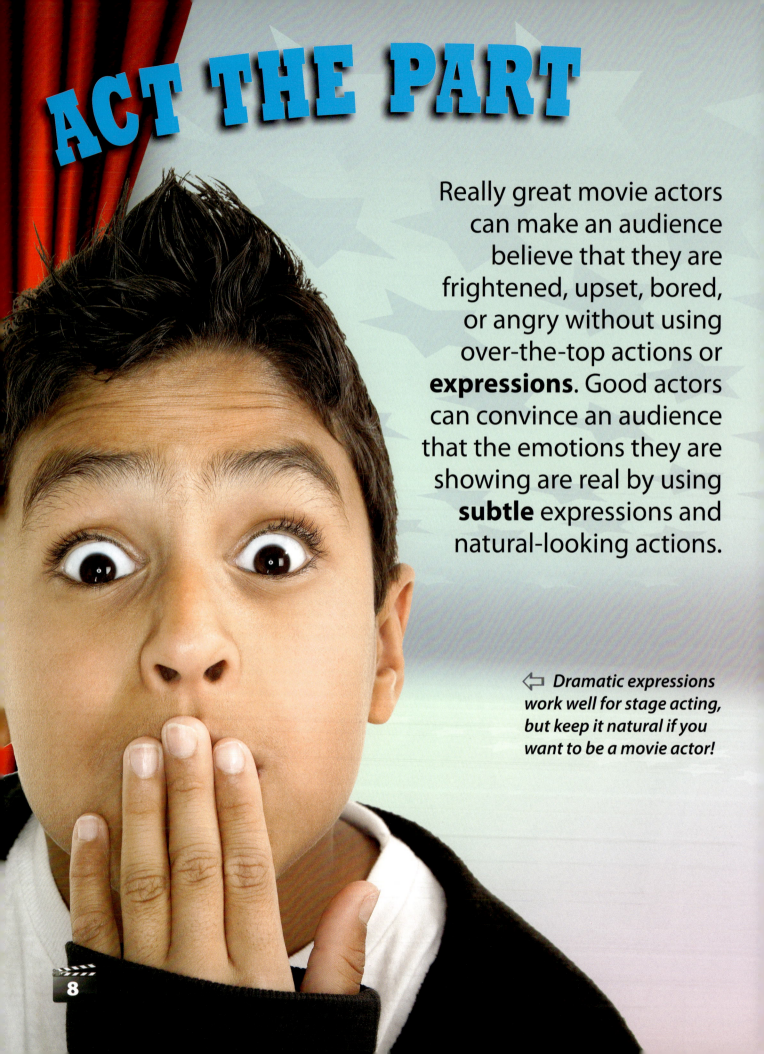

Really great movie actors can make an audience believe that they are frightened, upset, bored, or angry without using over-the-top actions or **expressions**. Good actors can convince an audience that the emotions they are showing are real by using **subtle** expressions and natural-looking actions.

⇐ *Dramatic expressions work well for stage acting, but keep it natural if you want to be a movie actor!*

Practice and timing

Work on your acting skills by practicing a whole range of acting styles. It's really important to work on your timing, too. You'll need to be able to say the right line at the right moment, especially in **comedy** movies.

⇨ *If you can dance, you may get a role in a musical movie.*

BE A STAR

All-around star

To give yourself the best chance of success, you'll need to learn to dance and sing, too. You can then act in both "straight" movies and dance and musical **productions**.

SCREEN TEST

Whether you're trying for a part in a school play, a movie, or a TV show, you will need to be ready long before you get to the audition. The audition is when you perform in front of a casting director in the hope that he or she will give you a part.

⇨ *Put lots of energy into your audition. This is your chance to impress!*

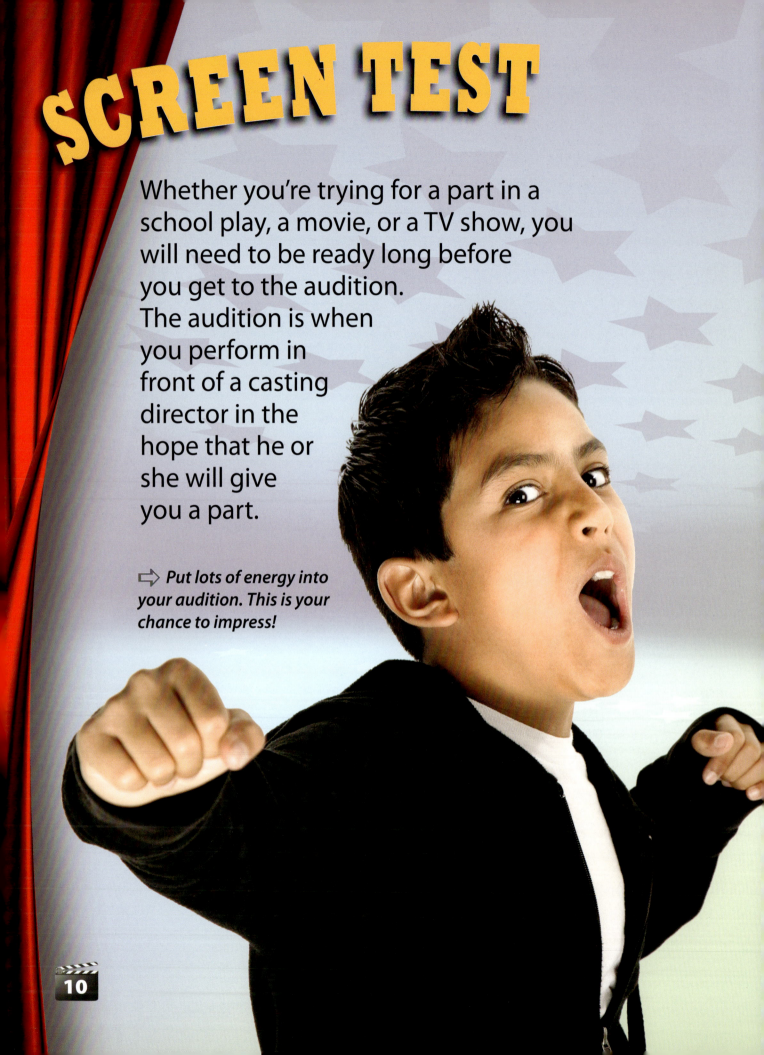

At the audition

A filmed audition is called a **screen test**. This is your big chance to shine:

- Wear medium to dark colors rather than white, as they work better on camera.

- Be prepared to speak in a different **accent**. Show off your acting range to the director.

- Be ready to make up words or simple actions on the spot.

⬆ *Take time to get your headshot just right and let your personality shine through in the photograph.*

BE A STAR

Get a good headshot

All casting directors will want to see a portrait photograph of your head and a short, written description of who you are. A bad photo could ruin your chances. It could even mean you don't get asked for an audition at all.

REMEMBER!

Once you have been given a movie part, your next step will be to learn your lines. This is very important. A great "take" (the filming of a small part of a movie) will be spoiled if someone forgets what to say halfway through! It is worth taking the time to practice your lines until you feel that you are word perfect.

⇐ *Read your script once more before you film a scene to help you to remember your lines.*

Repeat after me

Different people learn their lines in different ways. You will have to read your **script** over and over again. Walk around the room as you read it out loud.

Act it out

Ask your family to help by listening as you say your words, or by taking other parts in the script so you get to know your **cues**.

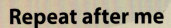

Listen carefully

Once you know your lines, listen to the other actors. That way, your lines will become a reply to their lines and sound more natural.

⬇ *You can act out a scene with your mom or dad to help you learn your lines.*

13

PEOPLE WATCHING

Watch people's **body language** as often as you can. It gives away what they are really feeling. Study what they do with their hands when they're bored, nervous, or shy. Watch how people behave when they are angry or upset. Notice their expressions and the way that they move. You can use these actions when you act.

⇩ *When you act, you use your voice, face, and body movements to show feelings.*

Write a list

Watch and listen to strangers and people you know. Write down as many words as you can to describe their voices and actions.

➡ *Keep a "people" notebook to write down how people behave.*

Listen and learn

When people talk, their voices show how they are feeling. People talk more loudly when they are angry, and smile as they talk when they are happy. Hear how people's voices change as their mood changes. Try to copy the different styles of speech.

BE INSPIRED!

Which actors most make you want to take up acting? It's fun to watch lots of movies and TV shows to see how actors play their parts. Try to watch all types, from comedy and **action movies** to serious **drama**.

Believe me!
Watch the same actor playing different parts to see if he or she plays them in a similar way. Do you believe in the character that the actor is playing?

⇨ *Will Smith has played both serious roles and funny parts in his many movies.*

Shut your eyes!
The voices of cartoon characters are spoken by actors. The next time you watch a cartoon, shut your eyes and listen to the way the actors speak their lines. They have to do all the hard work with just their voices and no movements at all.

← *Actor Mike Myers changed his accent to record the voice of Shrek.*

BE A STAR

Your favorites
A casting director may ask you about your favorite actors. Be prepared to say who you like and why you like them.

TALK THE TALK

Are you good at copying accents from around the country or around the world? Some people find it easy, while others have to work at it.

Don't be shy

Be brave when you try out a new accent, and don't give up if it doesn't sound right the first time. Your first attempts are bound to be off-target, but if you throw yourself into it, you will improve!

➡ *Take turns with your friends talking in a different accent. It's fun!*

Work at it!

- Listen to recordings of people from the same place as your character.

- Copy their exact words, and say them in the same way. Learn to feel where your tongue is as you speak.

- Use the same tongue and mouth shapes to attempt new words.

- Don't be afraid to try and fail, and try again.

⬇ *Record your accents, then listen to yourself to see how you sound.*

THE MOOD

Many actors believe in **Method acting**. This is playing a part as if you really are the character. Method actors imagine how they would feel if they were in the same situation as their character. They ask themselves, "What if this were really happening to me?"

Find out about feelings

Method actors often spend time talking to people who, in real life, have had the same experiences as their movie character. The actors then use the information to play their movie roles.

⇦ *Think of something that makes you feel really happy. Try to recreate the feeling when you act.*

Stanislavski

Many acting methods used today were developed by the director and actor Konstantin Stanislavski, sometimes called the "father of Method acting."

Strong feelings

Can you show more than one strong feeling, or emotion, at the same time? Think about how you feel when your mom is yelling at you. Sure, you might be mad at her, but you also know how much you love her, and you probably feel guilty for making her feel so angry. Practice showing more than one mood at the same time.

⇦ *Lowering your head and putting your hands on your hips can help to show anger.*

AND, CRY!

Many people would agree that crying on camera is really hard. So, how do you produce actual tears? Actors use different tricks to cry on screen in a way that seems natural and believable to the audience.

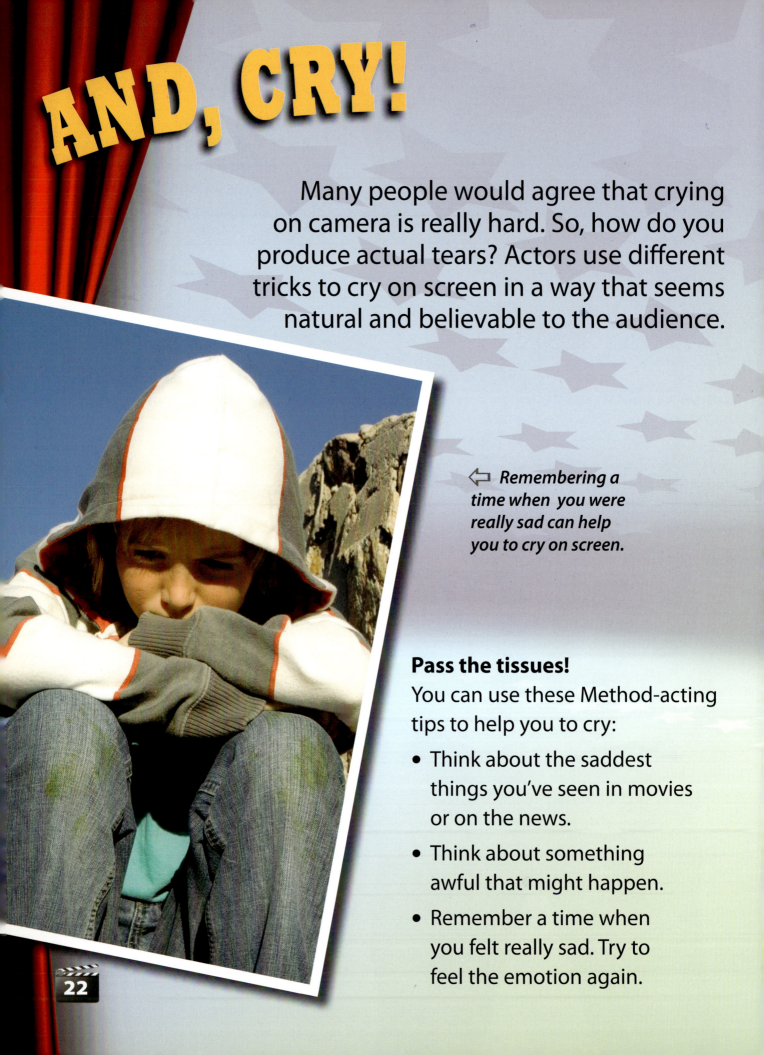

⇐ *Remembering a time when you were really sad can help you to cry on screen.*

Pass the tissues!

You can use these Method-acting tips to help you to cry:

- Think about the saddest things you've seen in movies or on the news.

- Think about something awful that might happen.

- Remember a time when you felt really sad. Try to feel the emotion again.

Real tears

Being able to cry in front of the camera is an important skill to master. Movie directors often zoom in with the camera to show an actor crying, so the tears must look real!

⇩ *A movie camera can zoom up close to show tears.*

SEE FOR YOURSELF

Many actors refuse to watch their own work on screen, but when you are just starting out, it can be useful. Use a cell phone or video camera to record yourself at home and judge your own performance.

⇦ *When you are acting, think about how it would feel if you were really being bullied.*

Watch it back

Choose a subject, such as bullying, to act out, and think about what might happen to each of the characters. Act out a scene on your own or with a friend. Make up the lines as you go along. This is called improvising. If you can, record your scene and play it back.

Does it look real?

Pretend you have been asked to make a TV commercial for a household item. Record your scene. When you watch it back, do you look natural, or do you look like you're acting?

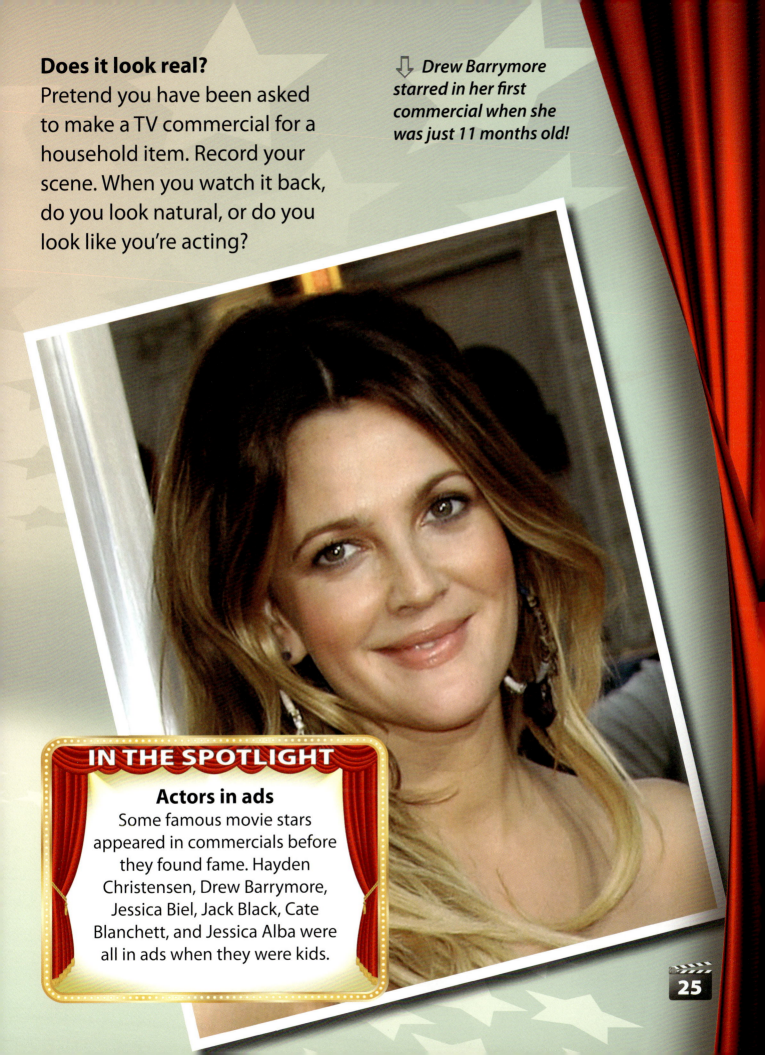

⇩ *Drew Barrymore starred in her first commercial when she was just 11 months old!*

IN THE SPOTLIGHT

Actors in ads

Some famous movie stars appeared in commercials before they found fame. Hayden Christensen, Drew Barrymore, Jessica Biel, Jack Black, Cate Blanchett, and Jessica Alba were all in ads when they were kids.

GET OUT THERE

It is really important that you do as much acting as you can. That way, you can tell a casting director about your work. You will also learn all about the art of acting and following direction, and, most important, get better every time!

⇦ *Vanessa Hudgens was in several local productions before she auditioned for TV parts.*

IN THE SPOTLIGHT

Tisdale and Hudgens
Both Ashley Tisdale and Vanessa Hudgens started acting in local productions. Vanessa got a fee of $50 for being a munchkin in *The Wizard of Oz*!

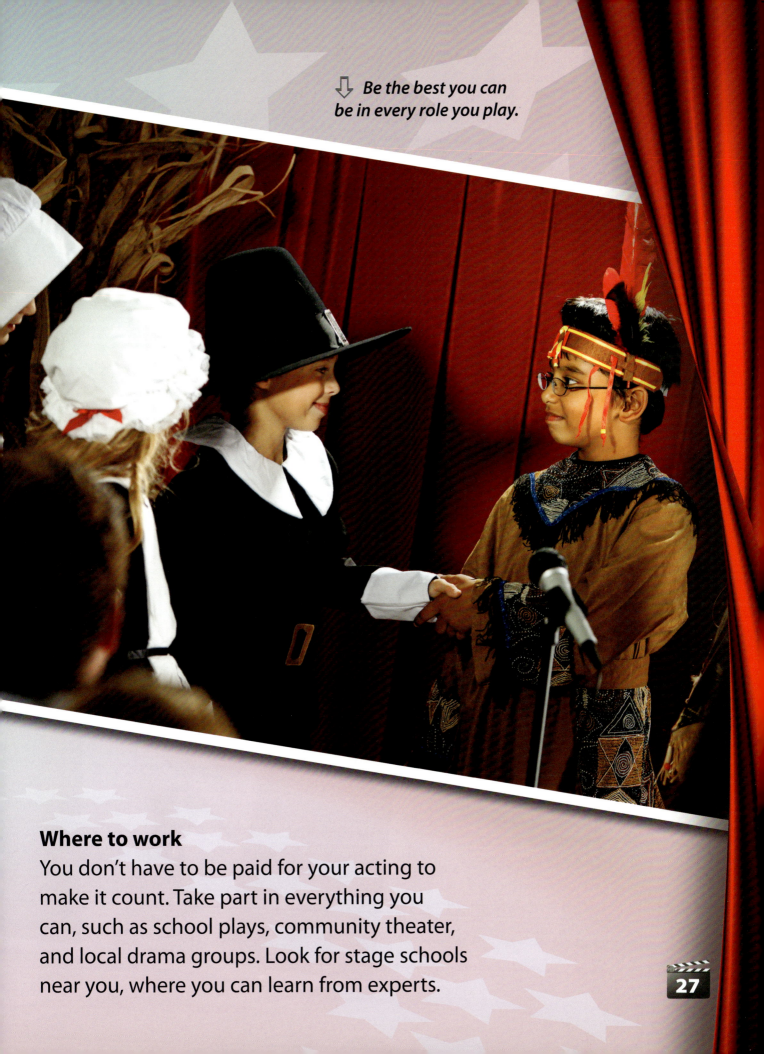

Be the best you can be in every role you play.

Where to work

You don't have to be paid for your acting to make it count. Take part in everything you can, such as school plays, community theater, and local drama groups. Look for stage schools near you, where you can learn from experts.

MEET THE AGENTS

An agent handles the business side of things for an actor. He or she knows about fees, contracts, working conditions, and the legal side of being a child actor.

Do you need an agent?

If you want to be an actor, you should consider having an agent, even if you don't have work yet. An agent will be able to put your name forward for screen tests. Many casting directors contact all the agents they know when they are looking for a child actor to play a part.

⇨ *Martin Scorsese, one of the world's greatest directors, worked with child actor Asa Butterfield in the movie* Hugo.

IN THE SPOTLIGHT

Zac Efron's wise words

"In the back of my mind, I can never forget this could be gone tomorrow. The chances of succeeding in this business are slim to none. You have to put in the work, you can never be satisfied, and never take it for granted."

⇨ *Zac Efron's drama teacher recommended him to a local agent when she saw how talented he was.*

29

GLOSSARY

accent
(AK-sent) The way in which a person from a particular area or country speaks.

action movies
(AK-shuhn MOO-veez) Movies that are packed with exciting events, such as chases.

auditions
(ah-DIH-shunz) Short performances given by an actor that tests whether he or she is right for a part.

body language
(BAH-dee LANG-gwij) Body movements or positions that show how you are feeling.

comedy
(KAH-meh-dee) A funny movie or play.

commercial
(kuh-MER-shul) An advertisement for a product on radio or TV.

cues
(kyooz) Words or actions that tell an actor when to speak or move.

drama
(DRAH-muh) A play or movie, usually a serious one.

expressions
(ik-SPREH-shunz) Showing feelings through the look on your face.

menthol tear stick
(MEN-thawl TEER STIK) A wax stick that you dab on your skin below your eye. The menthol smell makes real tears form.

Method acting
(MEH-thud AK-ting) Feeling the way the character feels, and acting that way.

productions
(pruh-DUK-shunz) Movies, plays, musicals, dance shows, or TV shows.

recording contract
(ri-KAWR-ding KON-trakt) An agreement between an artist and a record company that the artist will record a song and the record company will sell it.

screen test
(SKREEN TEST) At a screen test an actor performs in front of a movie camera to test whether he or she is right for a part.

script
(SKRIPT) The words of a movie, play, TV show, or commercial.

subtle
(SUHT-l) Delicate, not over the top or showy.

FURTHER READING

Bany-Winters, Lisa. *Funny Bones: Comedy Games and Activities for Kids*. Chicago, IL: Chicago Review Press, 2002.

Bedore, Bob. *101 Improv Games for Children and Adults*. Alameda, CA: Hunter House, 2004.

Belli, Mary Lou and Dinah Lenney. *Acting for Young Actors*. New York: Back Stage Books, 2006.

Friedman, Lise. *Break a Leg!: The Kid's Guide to Acting and Stagecraft*. New York: Workman Publishing Company, 2002.

Levy, Gavin. *112 Acting Games: A Comprehensive Workbook of Theatre Games for Developing Acting Skills*. Colorado Springs, CO: Meriwether Publishing, 2005.

WEBSITES

For web resources related to the subject of this book, go to: www.windmillbooks.com/weblinks and select this book's title.

INDEX